YOUNG SPIRITS

Edited By Lynsey Evans

First published in Great Britain in 2024 by:

Young Writers
Remus House
Coltsfoot Drive
Peterborough
PE2 9BF
Telephone: 01733 890066
Website: www.youngwriters.co.uk

All Rights Reserved
Book Design by Ashley Janson
© Copyright Contributors 2023
Softback ISBN 978-1-83565-137-7

Printed and bound in the UK by BookPrintingUK
Website: www.bookprintinguk.com
YB0577A

FOREWORD

For Young Writers' latest competition This Is Me, we asked primary school pupils to look inside themselves, to think about what makes them unique, and then write a poem about it! They rose to the challenge magnificently and the result is this fantastic collection of poems in a variety of poetic styles.

Here at Young Writers our aim is to encourage creativity in children and to inspire a love of the written word, so it's great to get such an amazing response, with some absolutely fantastic poems. It's important for children to focus on and celebrate themselves and this competition allowed them to write freely and honestly, celebrating what makes them great, expressing their hopes and fears, or simply writing about their favourite things. This Is Me gave them the power of words. The result is a collection of inspirational and moving poems that also showcase their creativity and writing ability.

I'd like to congratulate all the young poets in this anthology, I hope this inspires them to continue with their creative writing.

CROSSWORD

CONTENTS

Ardeley St Lawrence CE (VA) Primary School, Ardeley

Annabelle Krieger (9)	1
Chloe Wilkinson (9)	2
Ella Large (9)	3

Carrickmannon Primary School, Ballygowan

Reuben Ormerad (10)	4
Harry Harper (9)	6
Ella Craig (10)	7
Charlie McClintock (9)	8

Ruthin School, Ruthin

Harry Kenwright (12)	9
Grace Beech (12)	10

Salisbury Manor Primary School, Chingford

Eden Joscelyne (9)	11
Malaika Douglas (9)	12
Hamzah Abdillahi (10)	14
Ra-Moses Khelladi Taylor (9)	15
Savannah-Lyn Stewart (9)	16
Moira Steward (9)	17
Jayda Opoku Mensah (9)	18
Nicholas Calverley (9)	19
Ismaeel Hussain (9)	20
Omari Sesay (9)	21

Shaftesbury Primary School, Forest Gate

Navanshi Saxena (9)	22
Kavya Grover (9)	24
Dhyana Patel (9)	26
Amanah Mohammed (9)	27
Bilaal Aweis (9)	28

St Benedict's Junior School, London

Tazmin Rege (10)	29
Alex Zoumidou (11)	30
Sasha Norman (9)	32
Uma Sidhu (10)	34
Isla Levy (8)	36
George Bigland (11)	38
Sophia Norman (10)	40
Olly Hird (10)	42
Anaiah Majumder (8)	44
Yiming Zhong (10)	46
Freddie Codrington (11)	48
Danicka Eloise Hansen (8)	50
Orlando Pieralisi (10)	51
Viren Mathias (10)	52
Matteo Hanna	53
Adele Pieralisi (8)	54
Finnbar McQuillan Visintini (10)	55
Amelia Tombs (8)	56
Che Whitton (10)	58
Olivia Chatterjee (8)	59
Althea Hodge (8)	60
Jayen Gupta (9)	62
Diego Uribe (11)	64
Chloe Renaud (8)	66

Name	No.
Eleanor Hacking (8)	67
Ruby Harridge (9)	68
Leo Johnson (10)	70
Timur Khan (9)	71
Isabella Bernard (7)	72
Grace Howard (7)	73
Abi Langford (10)	74
Maia Amodu (9)	75
Otis Monaghan (10)	76
George Girgis (11)	78
William Johnson (7)	79
Damon Chavda (10)	80
Mikey Oldland (11)	81
Sofia Mihajloska (8)	82
Sienna Hall (9)	83
Zoeya Ahmed (9)	84
Finn Maguire (8)	85
Parth Rupani Jagtiani (8)	86
Eska Harris (7)	87
Florence Wiley (8)	88
Harry Campbell (10)	89
Anthony Sherlock (10)	90
Alasdair Lagan (10)	91
Joey Horgan (7)	92
Mikey Horgan (8)	93
Darcie Marron (7)	94
Dylan Avella (10)	95
Jenni Bosher (11)	96
Shay Patel (9)	98
Aiden Yihan Yuan (10)	99
Rehmat Kaur Azad (8)	100
Freya Kennedy-Alexander (8)	101
Owen Byrne (7)	102
Vihaan Mathias (9)	103
Reuben Adebutu (10)	104
Oliver Playle (7)	105
Isobel Oldland (8)	106
Yuika Naganuma (7)	107
Jamie Marshall (7)	108
Leo Mehrabi (7)	109
John Khadouri (8)	110
Luca Brathwaite (9)	111
Aariyan Fofaria (7)	112
Theo Joannou (7)	113
Noah Khatibi (9)	114
Archie Hird (7)	115
Aiden Maugham (7)	116
Mila Patel (7)	117
Yunlie Li (8)	118
Olivia Oke (8)	119
Elysia Papathanasiou (9)	120
Fintan Avella (8)	121
Lydia Johnson (7)	122
Rufus Wilson (8)	123
Zak Vosser (9)	124
Wolfie Ashman (7)	125
Charlie Goodridge (10)	126
Millie Scambler (10)	127
Afonso Gomes (8)	128
Ashwin Shah (8)	129
Taran Khera (9)	130
Raj Sidhu (10)	131
Jackson Harris (10)	132
Alessia McQuillan Visintini (10)	133
Rayan Serroukh (9)	134
Marcus Lee (10)	135
Carlotta Vannuccini (11)	136
Mark Pantea (10)	137
Letlotlo Wanjau (10)	138
Lucas Nossa (10)	139
Lisa Stoilovska (10)	140
Anastasia Norman (10)	141
Zac Bernard (10)	142
George Knight (10)	143
Leandro Craigen (11)	144
Niamh Kelly (9)	145
Olivia Lucas-Garner (9)	146
Maryam Alnajjar (9)	147
Aran Virdi (9)	148
Imogen Tringali (7)	149
James Giles (10)	150
Nathaniel Hodge (9)	151
Kayden Yip (10)	152
Maria Bizrah (8)	153
Vivaan Agarwal (9)	154
Frida Blanco (9)	155

Kenshiro Said (11)	156
Freya Hughes (10)	157
George Hacking (11)	158

Stanton Community Primary School, Stanton

Annalise Sharpe (10)	159
Jesse Brown (9)	160
Mia Preston (10)	162
Freddie Smith (11)	163
Joshua Smith Kerry (10)	164
Albie Bryant-Howe (10)	165
Dylan Policarpio (8)	166
Jessica Yeandle (10)	167
Lilah Cross (9)	168
Harry Cooper (10)	169
Darcey Marshall (8)	170
Layla Turner (9)	171
Ava-Leigh Russell Howllet (9)	172
Taylor Glass (10)	173
Reece Cannings (8)	174
Chelsea Dore (10)	175
Rex Cooper (10)	176
Caitlin Goodridge (9)	177
Finlay Ketcher (8)	178
Freddie Olney (8)	179
Bailey Daniel Thomas Hazelton (10)	180
Isabelle Steed (9)	181
James Hope (10)	182
Esmie O'Reilly (11)	183

Stapleford Abbotts Primary School, Stapleford Abbotts

Bonnie Jo Randall Jackson (10)	184
Lucas Pitcher (9)	186
Ava-Lea Brimacombe (9)	187
Sienna Ippoliti (8)	188
Talulah-Rose Adams-Smith (8)	189
Dervis Maraslioglu (7)	190
Winnie Duffy (10)	191
Teddy McAniskey (10)	192

Olivia Pitcher (11)	193
Isla West (8)	194
Oliver Dockerill (9)	195
Cauã Santos (8)	196
Isla Ray Hartley (7)	197
Freddie Jake Goddard (10)	198
Olivia Carle (7)	199
Ellie Eastwell (8)	200
Elsie-May Mesher (9)	201
Rosie Violet Rawson (8)	202
Jonny Ansett (7)	203
Jenson Man (9)	204
Riley Van Haaren (10)	205
Owen (8)	206
Mia (8)	207
Ayla Sonmez (9)	208

The Coppice Primary School, Hollywood

Beatrix Johnson (7)	209

THE POEMS

Me!

I love nature so I care for lots of animals,
Like cats, rats, dogs, hamsters, guinea pigs, mice and snakes.
Try to guess my name
I'll describe myself and you shall guess my name,
I love checking things out and the first letter of my name is A.
Okay so have an idea?
My name starts with the letter A.
So I love nature and the second letter of my name is N
So do you have a clue yet?
And what's next you ask
Oh, it's another N!
Do you have an idea?
Ann, no it's not Ann
Take another A, no my name is not Anna
There's a Belle then join them together, it's Annabelle!

Annabelle Krieger (9)
Ardeley St Lawrence CE (VA) Primary School, Ardeley

All About Me

The girl is happy,
She likes to run in the grass.
She is playful but cuddly
And she likes to go for walks.

Do you know her name?
It begins with C.
Do you know?
It's Chloe!

Chloe Wilkinson (9)
Ardeley St Lawrence CE (VA) Primary School, Ardeley

All About What I Like In My Life

E legant in dancing and swimming,
L oving and caring for my friends and my dog,
L ucky with my family and friends,
A rt, I love so much, I always ask to create.

Ella Large (9)
Ardeley St Lawrence CE (VA) Primary School, Ardeley

This Is Me Rap

My name's Reuben, I'm ten
I like turtles
I'm a great superfan, fast as a cheetah
Always getting in the way as a football defender
One thing about my family, my dad's so fussy about my hair.

I like red
I like red sauce, it's my life
Hating tomatoes, loving WWE
It's my life
But the base is hard, loving life
Just moved to Ballygowan
Unpacking, boring
But playing football represents me
Supporting Man City, good! Yours?

My family calls me American Kid
I love all things from America
Basketball, Feastables, Prime!
My birthday is on the thirteenth of October
Can't wait to get money

Loving going home from school
Playing Royal Rumble
Thirty WWE figures, love it

Dreaming to be in the police with a K9
Love to watch Hudson and Rex and Death in Paradise
Squirtle, love him, collect Pokémon cards
And football cards
I love cars and going fast
One of my biggest fears is flying
Or going in a boat
My favourite football player is KDB

Go get the baseball cap
Go to Linfield matches, support Lions
Love Ulster and Ireland
Going to Carrickmannon PS
In the football team and tag rugby
My favourite basketball team is Chicago Bulls
Loving playing and wearing the jerseys
This is me!

Reuben Ormerad (10)
Carrickmannon Primary School, Ballygowan

This Is Me

T o this day, I've loved sport
H i, my name is Harry and I'm from Belfast
I don't like maths, but people say I'm good at it
S ometimes I run with my dad

I also like playing video games
S ome of my friends live quite close. So I'm always playing with them

M ostly I play football, sometimes hockey
E very time I go outside, I'm playing football.

Harry Harper (9)
Carrickmannon Primary School, Ballygowan

My Dog Teddy

Teddy in the air
Teddy everywhere
You can even smell his hair from anywhere!
He's tiny like a pup, not a mare
He has tiny legs and fluffy hair
Big long ears, you can see them from anywhere
When he goes too rough, my mum takes care
He growls like a bear
It's probably just to scare
He just misses his mum, I know it's not fair
But I will take care
Of the big Teddy bear.

Ella Craig (10)
Carrickmannon Primary School, Ballygowan

Charlie

C harlie is my name.
H i, what's your name?
A nna Sophia is my sister.
R ugby is my favourite sport.
L osing is something I can't do.
I love drawing too!
E nd of the poem this is.

This is me!

Charlie McClintock (9)
Carrickmannon Primary School, Ballygowan

Uninteresting

H onestly, I don't know why you're reading this, I'm so uninteresting it's not even funny.
A ctually though, if you keep reading, you'll fall asleep out of sheer boredom.
R eally? You're still reading?
R ealistically, you should've stopped at "A".
Y ou're a nosy one aren't you!

'K ay... fine, I'll say a little about myself.
E specially on 'N'.
N ot "N"! I meant 'W'!
W rong again! I meant 'R'!
R ight, I can't think of any more excuses, so here goes:
I am Harry Kenwright and I have,
G ot a German Shepherd named Duke and I,
H ate babies that cry on flights.
T hat's it.

Harry Kenwright (12)
Ruthin School, Ruthin

Grace Beech

ManGo is the best fruit ever.
HorRor films are amazing.
I love to wAlk at night.
The best holiday is Christmas... obviously!
I adore monEy.

Bugs are disgusting.
Waking up Early is horrible.
SweEts taste absolutely vile.
The Colour orange burns my eyes.
I wholeheartedly despise Homework.

Grace Beech (12)
Ruthin School, Ruthin

Joscelyne The Joker

I put glue on people's chairs,
I put a fart cushion on my teacher's chair,
But then no one cares,
I started to run up the stairs,
Putting chocolate in people's pears,
Ewww, no one cares!
Ice cream!
Oh no, someone said I scream!
I scream in my dream,
When I used to be a teen,
When I was in a team,
When they were all mean,
By what I've seen,
I used to be supreme.

Eden Joscelyne (9)
Salisbury Manor Primary School, Chingford

Malaika Ruby Rude

M y teacher is very nice.
A untie loves to take me swimming.
L ove yourself.
A cashia is my favourite cousin.
I love chicken wings.
K FC is delicious.
A Wednesday is my favourite day.

R ude little girl at times.
U ses good fashion.
B eautiful at dancing.
Y ellow is her favourite.

M arvellous.
U sual.
M y mum loves me.

Rude
My cousin is rude sometimes
She dresses really fly.
When she has to go
To the front of the class

And read
She gets really shy.
She gets a lil attitude
When she does her hair
But I just ignore it
I don't really care.

Malaika Douglas (9)
Salisbury Manor Primary School, Chingford

Football

I like football
Especially when you score
You will end with money
And won't end poor
You have to kick the ball in the goal
And don't kick it slow
Or it isn't a goal
When it comes to half-time
You switch sides
You will have a break
And could drink lime
You kick in another goal
And it will go in
If you don't kick it low.

Hamzah Abdillahi (10)
Salisbury Manor Primary School, Chingford

Biscuits

B iscuits are very tasty and I like to eat them
I like chocolate digestives
S o I go to the shop
C an you buy me some biscuits?
U nderstand that they are the best
I can have biscuits every day
T hey are so incredible, every time I eat them, I get a rush of joy.

Ra-Moses Khelladi Taylor (9)
Salisbury Manor Primary School, Chingford

My Birthday

B irthday is the day I was born
I love my birthday
R eceive presents
T hank you Mum and Dad
H appy birthday
D ecorations on my birthday
A nnouncement, it's my birthday!
Y ay, it's my birthday.

Savannah-Lyn Stewart (9)
Salisbury Manor Primary School, Chingford

Moira

M agnificent
O dd
I ntelligent
R ebel
A mazing

S mart
T errific
E xtraordinary
W icked
A mbitious
R espect
D emanding.

Moira Steward (9)
Salisbury Manor Primary School, Chingford

Alphabet And Numbers

The alphabet starts with ABC
Then ends with XYZ

You can count to 123
But never to infinity

Say my name with a J
Then wrap it up with an A

Count up to infinity
Tricked you, hehehe.

Jayda Opoku Mensah (9)
Salisbury Manor Primary School, Chingford

What Am I?

N aughty
I ncredible
C ool
H umorous
O dd
L oved
A cceptable
S uper.

Nicholas Calverley (9)
Salisbury Manor Primary School, Chingford

What Am I?

I ntelligent
S mart
M iracle
A ngel
E xcellent
E xcited
L egend.

Ismaeel Hussain (9)
Salisbury Manor Primary School, Chingford

I Am King

K ing
I ntelligent
N icest boy you will ever meet
G rateful.

Omari Sesay (9)
Salisbury Manor Primary School, Chingford

This Is Me Navanshi - A Dreamweaver!

This is me,
Na-van-shi.
I'm just a nine-year-old child,
With boundless imagination that goes wild.

I strive to fill my days with cheer,
As each passing year draws near.
I share this poem with all my love,
To the world and beyond, like a soaring dove.

I feel a little worry deep inside,
Like butterflies in my tummy, they hide.
They flutter and dance in a hurry,
But I won't let them make me sorry.

I'm full of hobbies and high spirits,
Singing and dancing, my favourite merits.
I love to learn new things each day;
They'll guide me as I grow, in every way.

I dream of being an explorer who is bold,
Travelling the world, in stories untold.
I'll be having a great delight, and not a single fright,
I'll discover new places from morning 'til night.

I dream of being Supergirl doc,
Saving lives around the clock.
With my stethoscope, I'll be a pro,
Helping people wherever I go.
Adventures and smiles, my life will be bright,
As a life-saving doctor, I'll do it just right.

This is me,
Na-van-shi.
Time to wave and say goodbye,
But don't worry, time can fly.
We'll meet again, oh so soon,
Beneath the shining, joyful moon.

Navanshi Saxena (9)
Shaftesbury Primary School, Forest Gate

A Girl In The Mirror

Can you see what I can see?
A girl in the mirror is looking at me,
She looks quite short with her frizzy hair,
I will talk to her when I go over there,

She is slim and dainty in her shape,
But not as skinny as a piece of tape,
Her twinkling, brown eyes below her thick, black brow,
An angel at first sight with her undeniable glow,

This chirpy nine-year-old has tiny rosebud lips,
But her hairband does not always match her clips,
Now let's talk about her personality, kind and sweet.
But wait up, this girl's story is not yet complete.

The most sensitive girl you will meet on Planet Earth,
Crying had been her type of emotion since her birth,

If you want to meet her, she is sitting right in front of you,
Hi, my name is Kavya and all of the above is true.

You will notice, I can be peculiar at different times,
But as you read, I can make some amusing rhymes,
With all that said, it is time to say goodbye,
I know you want to hear more, but please don't cry.

Kavya Grover (9)
Shaftesbury Primary School, Forest Gate

Hi, This Is Me, Dhyana

Hi, my name's Dhyana, I like school
I eat bananas, they taste very cool
Playing with my friends in the playground
We run all about like a bunch of monkeys

Hi, my name's Dhyana, I like school
I have a lot of friends, I think they are very cool!
A boy starts being funny and everybody laughs
Then a boy starts being funny and unfortunately, nobody laughs!

Hi, my name's Dhyana, I like school
I like to joke around with a circle that is round
If everybody saw my personality
They would laugh like a clown!

Hi, my name's Dhyana, I like school
Let's end this now with a joyful smile
When it's time to go, let's all say bye
Which means we say it right now!

Bye guys!

Dhyana Patel (9)
Shaftesbury Primary School, Forest Gate

All About Me!

Happy, sad and in-between,
Those are what make my singing gleam,
Soft, loud and in-between,
Those are what make my singing gleam!

Drawing, writing and singing three,
These are what make me me,
Happy, excited and full of glee,
These are what make me me!

Anime, cute and colouring always in the line,
These are what make my drawing mine,
Beautiful, a sight and always very fine,
These are what make my drawing mine!

Stories, shorts and written with a shine,
These are what make my writing mine,
Poems, paragraphs and always above fine,
Those are what make my writing mine!

Amanah Mohammed (9)
Shaftesbury Primary School, Forest Gate

I'm A Power Ranger

P ower
O bedience
W orking hard
E mbracing
R eally kind.

R emarkably helpful
A ngelic ideas
N ever give up
G ood to people
E ncouraging always
R eally nice
S pends time with those I love.

Bilaal Aweis (9)
Shaftesbury Primary School, Forest Gate

Terrific Tazmin

I am really kind, I have a keen mind.
I can make amends, that's why I have loads of friends.
I love singing, you would *never* find me whingeing.
I have a dog, his fur is the colour of a bog.
I am a cheeky girl, one day I hope to travel the world.
You'll love me from the start, my kindness fills up in my heart.

People know my name, I have a lion's mane.
I love to game but I am the same.
I am a good surfer, I also nurture.
I am very happy, I have been since I was in nappies.
My favourite pop star is Olivia Rodrigo, I have a friend called Diego, he is a bit of a freak-o.
I have a horse called Robyn, his favourite move is bobbing.
One day I hope to be an actor, though I would *never* drive a prop tractor.
This is me.

Tazmin Rege (10)
St Benedict's Junior School, London

Sport

Hi, my name is Alex, and I like to play sport,
But not on a court,
Something like a court,
Where I can shoot and cannot miss,
I hope you're thinking about football,
Because it's a very tough sport,
If you're wrong, then you might need to get taught,
Let me tell you about it,
You need a ball,
Try not to fall,
Dribble like a pro,
And then put on your show,
Do some skills and make the defender say, "Ahh!"
Pow! The ball is in the air,
Then in the back of the net,
Now you're a threat,
Celebrate like your pet,
Go crazy, you scored a goal,
Check on your toe,
Make sure it's not hurt,
Good, it's not,

Now back to your position,
Get your team promoted,
Have a cheer,
For next year,
In the league,
Some players are very antique,
But are still in the pro league,
Don't be scared,
Because you will get paired,
With a new team,
And a new theme.

Alex Zoumidou (11)
St Benedict's Junior School, London

This Is Me

I love drama
It makes me calmer
Ozzy and Timmy my cats are winners
I feed them chicken dinners

When I do the splits
My sisters flip
I'm always enthusiastic
When I do gymnastics

When I do badminton
My teachers never frown
I have a mother
But no brother

Two sisters and a fantastic father
My favourite fantastic friend
We stick together
And we're friends forever

At drama, I'm the drama queen
When I stand on a beam

I'm very keen
To do a cartwheel

I love sushi and cotton candy
It makes me happy
When it's shaped like a flower
I'm very eager just like a cheetah

I love dance
One day I will learn to prance
Sticky toffee pudding
Is good when it's cooking!

That is me!

Sasha Norman (9)
St Benedict's Junior School, London

This Is Me

We can agree to disagree,
But I am free.

I am a kaleidoscope of feelings, that you will find,
I'm nothing special, but I am kind.

Everyone else is addicted to drama,
However, I'm just a little bit calmer.

Selfishness leads other people the wrong way,
But it won't trick me, not today.

The old ways have changed,
The new ways are strange.

I think I'm quite powerful,
But I just try to be joyful.

Everyone else can think of me as forgetful or blonde,
However, I'm just not trying to bond.

Craziness is what people demonstrate,
But I won't lead myself into that brutal fate.

When a day is an atrocity,
I get back up courageously.

Each day I make a new creation,
Then I scream and jump around in elation.

Uma Sidhu (10)
St Benedict's Junior School, London

My Beloved Family

M y beloved family is the only thing I love, Maddox my brother the annoying one loves to play piano
Y ummy spinach spaghetti is my favourite with tomato sauce

F amily group hugs will remain warm and snug
A nd so will building forts in my room too
M y favourite dessert is Milky Bar so nice and sweet
I love drawing and doodling
L oving my kittens too
Y es I might be strange

I sla is my name
S o I will still remain

T his way
H olding balloons and popping party poppers
E verything is almost favourite of mine

B ut still I can do the things I don't do
E verything that I don't do is on my checklist
S o my family is my favourite still
T hat's all.

Isla Levy (8)
St Benedict's Junior School, London

My Seasons

When I am spring
I will canter in the sunlight
And will stare at the pink blossoms

I'd lend a bright smile
While I thank the generous
And say a kind word

I'd hold my friends' hands
If they were stuck in sinking sand
Because I am me

When I am summer
I'd chase the gold dragonflies
And surf on the waves

I'd bring all my friends
When I lay my lightning out
They'd return a smile

I'd try not to trip
And make sure not to hurt them
Because I am me

When I am autumn
I would sit on the dead leaves
And absorb the breeze

I'd lower in heat
When my friends are in fire
Because I am me

When I am winter
I'd freeze under the moonlight
And plead to the stars

George Bigland (11)
St Benedict's Junior School, London

This Is Me

Who am I?

Well, I'm bendy like a piece of paper,
Better than a professional baker,
I read and I game,
I leap and I keep.
Who am I?

I'm quick on my feet,
I stumble and I mumble,
I slip and trip,
You might think I'm clumsy, but no,
It's rare to be fair,
But who am I?

I'm super kind, super smart
And I care the most out of them all,
I'm a daydreamer and a pet owner at the same time,
I've got two little sisters,
One is a twin but I've got to admit, they're quite annoying,
But who am I?

I'm tidy and mighty,
Kittens are my jam,
Dogs are okay but not my favourite fam,
I am peaceful like a lamb,
Oh, I remember who I am.

Who I am,
Sophia.

Sophia Norman (10)
St Benedict's Junior School, London

My Happiness Recipe

I was happy, I am happy, I want to stay happy,
Like a face-stretched Cheshire cat, my smile is gappy,
I sing like a bird in flight, eyes closed without a care,
Happiness to me is about living life with flair,

I kick, I cycle, I jump, I laugh, I swim,
But I am lucky, a big chunk of my happiness comes from my family limb,
To stay happy you need to look after more than you,
The family, community and Earth needs its people to be its glue,

Giving back is an important thing,
If humans take all the time and act like their own king,
Chaos will spread like a sickness, from door to door,
And Cheshire smiles will be vacuumed from us all,

So be aware, be kind, and care for more than you,
And you will stay happy, be happy, always happy, never blue.

Olly Hird (10)
St Benedict's Junior School, London

Me, Myself, Anaiah

Me, is who I am,
Friendly, fantastic, awesome,
And wonderful, me.

I have a cousin who is just like me,
She says I'm supportive and calls me "Chatun Didi",
She loves wildlife, just like me,
We're pretty much a carbon copy.

I love my family,
And I am super dreamy,
I write stories,
I call it my story,
Me!

I am me,
Funny, silly, giggly me,
I love to dance,
And love to play in the sun all day.

I love to be me,
I'm friendly, lovely,

And oh so happy,
I am me.

I'm an absolute dog lover,
I'm passionate about my dreams,
And love to eat my greens,
Smart, intelligent, curious,
Cool, cute, yep that's me alright.

Anaiah Majumder (8)
St Benedict's Junior School, London

This Is Me

If I am the colour blue
The world is very true

If I am the colour green
I am somewhere in-between

If I am the colour gold
I feel very bold

If I am the colour bones
I will be singing different tones

If I am the colour silver
I will be a believer

If I am the colour yellow
You might hear me bellow

If I am the colour red
I would want to be in bed

If I am the colour rose
I will smell it with my nose

If I am the colour cherry
I will feel very merry

If I am the colour grape
I might act like an ape

If I am the colour moss
I feel like the boss

If I am all the colours
I do not feel like the others.

Yiming Zhong (10)
St Benedict's Junior School, London

All About Me

Millions of people live on this Earth,
Millions of people haven't found the love,
Lord God help us find the love.

My Earth is a football,
And the pitch is space,
The rugby balls are different planets,
And cricket balls are the asteroids.

We all are wonderful in our own ways,
To being kind, to being smart,
To being great at sports and a good team player,
To being grateful and loving.

I love life,
It is wonderful,
Nothing is bad,
Friends are great.

Sport is wonderful,
From scoring tries to saving penalties,
Smashing a ball for six or hitting a century,

All the ups and downs, losing to winning,
Finding friends to having fun.

Freddie Codrington (11)
St Benedict's Junior School, London

Mindfulness

D anicka is fun and amazing,
A nimals are cool and interesting,
N ote things down when I have ideas,
I nteresting things are amazing,
C heerful things are delightful,
K indness is the best in every single way,
A mazing family and friends.

I can do things,
S haring is fun, you will have more friends.

R elaxing is the best, you can do it every day,
E veryone is the best in every single way,
L aziness is relaxing,
A nything that is fun is good,
X ylophones are musical and fun,
I am the best,
N ice is the best,
G ratitude is the best and I can do it every day.

Danicka Eloise Hansen (8)
St Benedict's Junior School, London

Is This Me?

Who am I?
Will I be remembered?
Am I going to be praised?

When days are grey,
Will I choose to be yellow or blue?
Out of so many choices, is there one for me?

Will they know that all they see is just the tip of the iceberg?
Shall they know that I'm not what they think I am?
Do they know my opinions are different?

Who knows how to fill the hole in my heart?
How would they know of my other side
When it is hidden?

Just for being a special person,
Out of four billion others,
Will I ever be able to be me?

Will I make a difference?
Can I be me in front of others?
Or will I be shaped differently?

Orlando Pieralisi (10)
St Benedict's Junior School, London

All About Me

I am extraordinary, it is real what you see,
I like football, but I sometimes fall.
When I fall, I am not sad,
Because football makes me glad.

I like poems, they're fun to read,
In my mind, it's like growing a seed.
I like poems and this is no joke,
They make me laugh, I sometimes choke.

I am sporty, I love cricket,
I'm super because I get wickets.
I am talented, I play the piano,
If the piece is sad, I play a diminuendo.

I am Viren, I play chess,
If I lose it gets me a little stressed.
Whether I win or lose, the world can see,
What a fine young boy I am growing up to be.

Viren Mathias (10)
St Benedict's Junior School, London

All About Me!

This is me,
I like ice cream, it is very nice,
It also gives me loads of strife,
Rugby's my thing, it's very rough,
But I play contact not touch,
In tennis, I'm the best in town,
My opponents always leave with a frown,
At piano, I'm the master,
I train every day for my fingers to move faster,
I just moved to year five,
My teacher Mrs Gibson is the best one alive,
This is me, I'm as cheeky as a monkey,
In hide-and-seek people never find me,
When I'm happy my smile brightens up the mood,
Especially when I'm eating food,
I'm very brave, even in the night,
Nothing ever gives me a big fright.

Matteo Hanna
St Benedict's Junior School, London

Tiny Artist

I f I were a tiny artist

W ould have fun all day long
O nly when I get excited my paint would burst into a rainbow of fun
U nicycle of creativity
L ike a tiny artist
D o dangerous things like leaving my paint to dry overnight

B eing kind
E ven if they are rude

A rt, yes! A tiny bit of science, but more art
N ever give up

A lways kind
R eading and reading, yes!
T iny tiny bit of paint on my finger
I s everybody cheering for me?
S parkly always being me
T ired at the end of the day.

Adele Pieralisi (8)
St Benedict's Junior School, London

Feelings

This is me and I am not scared,
If people disrespect me, it's like I never cared

Sometimes I feel like a mighty soldier,
But other times, I feel like I've been flattened by a boulder

I feel like a songbird whose wings have been ripped off,
And at other times, I feel like a beautiful peacock who isn't scared to show off

I am a beautiful rose,
Until my petal is ripped off so someone can smell it with their nose

The mustard seed is one of the smallest seeds,
But when it grows up it becomes the biggest tree

From the smallest beginnings... and that is me!

Finnbar McQuillan Visintini (10)
St Benedict's Junior School, London

Christmas Day - A Shape Poem

I
love
Christmas,
The best time ever,
When the whole family
comes together,
Going up to Birmingham,
Where Nanny and Grandad,
Await, smiling, so happy to see us,
We put out the milk and carrots
and wait for the morning,
Then my cousins arrive
with their puppy,
Their puppy is lucky to be invited
to the Christmas crazy party,
I try to be responsible,
by making sure the puppy
doesn't eat the wrapping paper,

Then out comes the Christmas dinner,
That everyone worked hard on,
The puppy gets some beef,
And then we all open our presents,
What a laugh!

Amelia Tombs (8)
St Benedict's Junior School, London

A Spectacular Blip

A spectacular blip on the horizon
Determined to be something special
So let's be sentimental
A mix of nations across the seas
With mottled, milky coffee eyes and flecks of green
That is me!
I ask myself questions, what I am?
Who am I? Teeny? Tall? Slightly? Stoutly?
Too many questions need answering
But my thoughts are cancelling
A computer geek is what I could be
But anything more could be achieved!
I want to build empires
Work till I tire
Will I have to break myself
and ruin my health?
I think not
For I will rise to the top
and share my empire!

Che Whitton (10)
St Benedict's Junior School, London

Amazing Me!

T idy, fun, caring and kind
H aving lots of things going on in my mind
I am courageous and bold
S ometimes chilled, though sometimes cold

I am a scientist, this is me!
S mart as a parrot, talented as a bee

A mbitious and energetic
M y life is fantastic
A nd I love reading fiction
Z oos are incredible, robots I love because they malfunction
I am a sparkling diamond, bringing cheer everywhere
N o shoes under size thirty-two will fit my footwear
G o, go, go, sneak around like a snake.

Olivia Chatterjee (8)
St Benedict's Junior School, London

Dogs

They are funny,
Cute and sweet,
They're not very purry,
When walked they always lead.

Enjoy playing catch,
All seem to like me,
Against a cat, they're no match,
They can pee on a tree.

They're the cutest pet,
Nice and very cosy,
They need to see the vet
And are extremely nosy.

Enjoy sleeping in their bed,
Sometimes very sleepy,
Get a chance to rest their head,
Investigate when a door's creaky.

No way they see as much as you,
Can always cheer you up
But does a very, very, stinky poo,
Even when a pup.

Althea Hodge (8)
St Benedict's Junior School, London

My Wonderful Life

Sports is my thing,
I'm the cricket king.
I'm a football guy,
I never sigh.

I'm great at maths,
I love warm baths.
I make friends
To the very end.

My eyes are as dark as night,
I'm an unstoppable knight.
I reach an astronomical height,
It's an unimaginable sight.

I'm the best of the best,
I don't need rest.
I love gaming,
I'm always saving.

Bang, crash, smack,
I have lots of sacks.

My hair dances in the wind,
I'm a kind kid.

This is me!

Jayen Gupta (9)
St Benedict's Junior School, London

This Is Me

Who am I?
Who am I?
Some struggle to answer,
But only I know.

They think they know,
Who you are,
Others think ill of me,
Some might love me.

But nobody, not even I,
Can judge you,
You set your own story,
You know your path.

Words are my *ink*,
I am the pen,
Once the ink is on the paper,
My story is written.

My head is like spaghetti,
My thoughts, feelings

And emotions
In a clump and undecided.

Life is like,
A subway map,
You can go,
Down different paths.

Diego Uribe (11)
St Benedict's Junior School, London

Cats

Cats are fluffy and like to sleep, purr
They run and climb they scratch and claw
Cats look cute and curl up on your legs
They sometimes hiss and whack
When they are let out they dash and climb up a tree

Always they roll in catnip and go crazy
They sometimes don't want to hug
But that doesn't mean they hate you
They just slept bad
The cats are cuddly and adorable

These cats are kind but some of them are mean
So be careful not to have one of those
So now you know so much about them
Why don't you try to get one? They are so fun!

Chloe Renaud (8)
St Benedict's Junior School, London

My Family And Me

My family is the best,
Especially on Christmas Day,
They make me happy every single day,
They let me do lots of hobbies and things,
And on my birthday they make me laugh.
I love doing sports, skating, shopping, sewing and riding a Segway,
I also like reading, slugs, helping, snails,
I like dancing and acting even more things,
Things I like doing outside are riding my bike, scooting, skateboarding and rollerblading, and playing outside.
My birthday is not the best,
Christmas is better, so then everyone gets to open presents,
And it is a special day for everyone.

Eleanor Hacking (8)
St Benedict's Junior School, London

This Is Me

I am brave, I am bold,
Don't mess around with me,
Trust me, you'll be told.

I am cool, I am proud,
I will say it out loud,
I am kind, I am mischievous,
I am very courageous.

My hair is quite straight,
Believe me, I never hate,
Chocolate is my favourite treat,
It's amazing to eat!

My siblings are kind,
They have great minds,
They really do shine!

Hear me now,
I never get bored,

Write my name out many times,
I am great at making rhymes!

This is me.

Ruby Harridge (9)
St Benedict's Junior School, London

The Rap

Sport is my thing,
I'm a football king,
In English, I have multiple crowns,
Because the teacher never frowns,
In maths, I really know my stuff,
Because I never fluff,
I'm better than all the boys,
My correct answers hit like asteroids,
My friendships are super strong,
We could survive if we got smashed by King Kong,
I have outstanding bravery,
That can only be matched by my creativity,
I'm a first-place machine,
In rugby I always come clean,
I'm a house point monster,
My nickname is Leo the lobster.

Leo Johnson (10)
St Benedict's Junior School, London

My Fantastic Life

Yo, I'm in the house
This is all about me
And I love meat with broccoli
You see, I also love tea
Because you can get cake to take
And sit by the lake

I hate when I am late to school
It's just not cool
My favourite subject is art
I love riding on a trolley cart
I also buy tiny tarts at a mini-mart
I also have a nice big heart

I am a really good rugby player
But the worst sketcher
I also do Scouts
And I doubt Brussels sprouts
Now I need to say goodnight
So don't let the bedbugs bite.

Timur Khan (9)
St Benedict's Junior School, London

This Is Me!

T oday, I had a wonderful day because I made slime.
H alloween is my favourite day because I can trick or treat.
I love my teacher because he teaches me so much.
S ometimes when it is tempestuous weather, I have a sleepover with my cousins.

I ran as quick as a cheetah for cross country.
S ome of my favourite animals are a dog, cat and horse.

M y mum and dad make me happy every day.
E very Tuesday, I go to science and I love it, we make lovely stuff and my dad is always astonished.

Isabella Bernard (7)
St Benedict's Junior School, London

This Is Me

T his is a poem about me and I'm a healthy, happy girl,
H appy Halloween, it's time to celebrate, my favourite day is Halloween,
I learned that I am energetic and diligent,
S chool makes me feel amazing, I'm happy and excited,

I am so excited for my birthday, it's so fun!
S uper animals are my thing,

M y favourite one is a cute koala, my happy family looks after me and cares for me,
E urope is one of my family's continents, it's cool and super.

Grace Howard (7)
St Benedict's Junior School, London

This Is Me

Hi, so this is me...
I make enemies and look back at memories,
I fear bumblebees that chase me,
I keep myself relaxed, I drink lots of tea and coffee,
Yes, I have flaws and don't get applause,
I have a mother, father, and a brother,
I'm not sentimental nor very special,
My friends can tell the right from the wrong,
I can't,
I love the colour pink,
In my opinion, water is the best drink,
I like food, I can't chop wood,
I dance in the rain,
I'm not sure I have a brain.

Abi Langford (10)
St Benedict's Junior School, London

Who Am I?

I am as jumpy as a frog,
Calm as a dog,
As bright as the sun and full of fun,
I am confident, kind and considerate,
I'm a brave, bright, gorgeous girl,
I'm sporty and enjoy running,
I am benevolent and sweeter than strawberries,
I'm nice and bright with pretty eyes,
But when scared, anger comes, I need to run,
Afraid of being caught!
Anxiousness has already caught me,
But all I need to do is count to ten and blow all my worries away,
Now do you know who I am?
I am Maia Amodu.

Maia Amodu (9)
St Benedict's Junior School, London

Why?

I won't drink wine,
So come and dine,
With me and God,
No time to sob,
Or feel alright.

Who am I?
Why am I?
Who is God?
And who is not?
I'll think again and again,
Why?

Who am I?
I look into the sky,
And wonder why,
Why we have falls,
Why we go and play,
Why we sit and why we stand,
Just why?

I wonder why,
We have a sky,
And I wonder why we have to die,
Why we eat,
And why we sleep,
Just why?

Otis Monaghan (10)
St Benedict's Junior School, London

Who I Am

I love my family,
Who have been with me,
Football is the best,
That is why I am training,
I am really humble,
That is why I don't crumble,
I am still at the beginning of my life,
That is why I don't have much height,
I believe in God,
That is how I am religious,
I am really sporty,
But sometimes, I am really naughty,
I am Egyptian,
That is where my mum and dad are from,
I am friendly,
And I have a lot of friends,
I love my life,
So this is me!

George Girgis (11)
St Benedict's Junior School, London

This Is Me

T he teachers are really, really nice. I like the way they teach me so much stuff.
H appy and healthy I try to be when I play football.
I like watching football with my dad and playing football.
S arah is the name of my mum and she smells like a plum.

I like playing with my friends at breaktime.
S ugar and sweets are what my dad doesn't let me eat.

M y friend Andrew is also sad when I am.
E lephants are my dream thing to ride.

William Johnson (7)
St Benedict's Junior School, London

This Is Me

If I am nervous, my hands will shake
If I am annoyed, my anger will break

Causing anger and annoying my siblings
When I am annoyed, I imagine water rippling

I don't know my future, however I know my past
I can be odd and want things like a cast

Maybe I'll know someone with a divorce
Maybe I'll know someone who connects like a magnetic force

I want my name to be in the hall of fame
Or maybe I'll be a joyous character and stay the same.

Damon Chavda (10)
St Benedict's Junior School, London

Mikey

Name's Mikey, I'm makin' money,
I be the brain of the school, big brain,
School be easy and life be friendly, crikey!
When the Bees get three points, I get the tea, crikey!
I beat my foes on a bike, oh Mike!
Blackbelt in kung fu, ha ho!
I be captain IT, beep bop!
When all goes black, I go to the track!
First place! Yeehaw!
USA, UAE, been there, how about you? You?
Got the bucks for the PS5, how about you? You?
I made a poem about me, how about you? You?

Mikey Oldland (11)
St Benedict's Junior School, London

This Is Me

S tay cool!
O ptimistic me.
F orgive people.
I am the best I can be!
A lways be humble and kind.

T ell the truth.
H appiness is helpfulness!
E verywhere you go, kindness will show.

S haring is caring.
U nbelievable scores!
P ure passion.
E nthusiastic.
R adical!
S assy and smart.
T his is me!
A mazing world.
R ule the world!

Sofia Mihajloska (8)
St Benedict's Junior School, London

My Wonderful World

Hi it's Sienna, that's my name
I have a brother, a dad and a mum from Spain
For me, dancing is the best
Do you think I'm better than the rest?

I'm blonde, tall and wear glasses
My teacher thinks I work hard in classes
Netball is my favourite sport
I go running up and down the court

I'm very funny with lunatic friends
Our friendship will never come to an end
White chocolate is my favourite treat
It satisfies my stomach just to eat.

Sienna Hall (9)
St Benedict's Junior School, London

All About Me

I am a hockey player,
And I'm a bread maker,
I had a horsey,
And I'm sporty.

When my brother comes in my room, I am furious,
When I look in my sister's room, I am curious.

I have brown eyes,
And I am a spy,
My hair is curly,
And I come to school early.

I have a bear,
And I really care,
I am sporty,
Don't tell anyone, I am a little bit naughty.

I am a fan of the River Nile,
And I love Harry Styles.

Zoeya Ahmed (9)
St Benedict's Junior School, London

My Likes And Fears

I like jelly and ice cream,
I like video games too.
I'm terrified of spiders,
I'll hide in my room for days,
My favourite animal is a red panda,
Because they are so fluffy,
If I were an animal
I would be a hamster because they are so small,
My favourite sport is rugby,
Because it is so fun and rough,
I find it hard to control my sadness, anger and silliness too.
I do not like coffee, I do not like pepper.
I like to drink tea, I also like carrots.

Finn Maguire (8)
St Benedict's Junior School, London

The Fun Times

Hello! I am so funny and also shy,
I love playing with my friends and family all day and night.
When I play adventure games with my mum and dad,
They always want to play with me,
But I have to do my homework first.
I love my mum and dad,
They help me do my homework quickly,
And then we play video games and have lots of fun!
Then we have an amazing sleep,
And then there's a rising star called the sun.
Thank you for reading this, bye!

Parth Rupani Jagtiani (8)
St Benedict's Junior School, London

Eska's Poem

T his is an acrostic poem about me.
H alloween, my favourite day, is nearly here.
I 'm a seven-year-old sporty and fun girl.
S aturday is my favourite day because I have gymnastics.

I ndigo is my silly sister, I love her very much.
S nails are my favourite insects because they slither around.

M ondays we do hockey at school, I really enjoy it.
E ska is my name and it comes from Africa.

Eska Harris (7)
St Benedict's Junior School, London

Swimming

Finally the day has come! The day I have swimming lessons
My favourite day of the week
I love the feeling of stepping in the cleansed water
And diving into the magic world underneath it

I've dreamed that in the swimming pool
There is a secret crater far below
My swimming coach Rita is a fine lady
Teaching us butterfly and front crawl

After my lesson I go home to a yummy supper
I can't wait for swimming next week.

Florence Wiley (8)
St Benedict's Junior School, London

I Am Me

If I am pink
I bloom like a flower,
And if I am bright
I shine with power.

If someone is stuck
And needs a helping hand,
I will be green to help them
And in the end, feel grand.

If I lie in my bed,
I am probably red,
And when I am hungry
I will make some bread.

If I am yellow
I say black and yellow, bellow
I will watch the Bee Movie
With a groovy smoothie

Because I am me.

Harry Campbell (10)
St Benedict's Junior School, London

About Me

Hi, my name is Anthony, I like Sprite,
I wish I could drink it every night,
I play basketball every day,
Hoping I may become one of the best one day,

Loving everyone I see, it's my number one curiosity,
Looking at sharks makes my mind go boom,
Seeing my friends makes my happiness grow,
They call me McLaren because of how fast I am running,

I like eating steak for a break,
At school, for break, I eat apples, sadly not steak.

Anthony Sherlock (10)
St Benedict's Junior School, London

I Am Me

I am me,
I am me when I get home,
I can be free,
I walk along with my dog,
I have two cats,
One is fat and one is thin as a baseball bat,
I play videogames like a pro,
But my friend is better though,
I am me,
I am me,
I like to play rugby,
I do my work,
Every so often my brother goes berserk,
When I run my feet burn,
My bones churn,
But I am me,
I am me,
And this is my life.

Alasdair Lagan (10)
St Benedict's Junior School, London

This Is Me

T his is a poem all about me and I am happy.
H alloween is my spooky, scary time of year.
I 'm happy, healthy and the person I want to be.
S t Benedict's is the fantastic, brilliant school I go to.

I am happy and kind like everyone should be.
S ummer holiday is my favourite time of year.

M onkeys are my favourite animal.
E ating healthily helps you.

Joey Horgan (7)
St Benedict's Junior School, London

All About Me

I love football and rugby,
They are my favourite sports,
They are very cool,
Also, they are very fun,
They are my favourite, yes my favourite!
I love them so much,
I'm very good at them,
I have two siblings,
They are four and seven,
I love them,
I play football with my brother,
And I play in the garden with my sister,
My favourite food is pasta,
But it has to be gluten-free.

Mikey Horgan (8)
St Benedict's Junior School, London

This Is Me

T oday, I will be telling you all about me!
H i, my name is Darcie and I like to do fun things like dance
I like, yummy ice cream, it is just the best!
S o, what do you like? Yummy ice cream?

I like doing dancing and learning cool tricks.
S o, do you like learning cool tricks?

M y favourite food is pasta.
E nglish Is my favourite subject.

Darcie Marron (7)
St Benedict's Junior School, London

This Is Me

I don't like football,
I don't like rugby,
But I do like other things,
I fool around,
I faff around,
I love to cook; especially to bake.

You may think I look boring but I'm actually very fun,
Every day I stare in the mirror that's when you think I'm dull,
But I am actually thinking of potions and mud pies and all sorts of things,
So I think I'm rather fun.

Dylan Avella (10)
St Benedict's Junior School, London

I Am Me

A kennings poem

Scab picker
Lolly licker

Smoothie drinker
Good thinker

Bad burper
Slushy slurper

Pet owner
Big moaner

Big questioner
Big messenger

Verse two

Ugly crier
Good trier

Ice eater
Loud sleeper

Loud talker
Straight walker

Good sister
Not a listener

I'm a jester
I'm better.

Jenni Bosher (11)
St Benedict's Junior School, London

Halloween

Halloween what a brilliant thing,
Fun costumes, cool prizes, how much fun could it be,
Spiderwebs and pumpkins all around the house,
Surely nothing is better than that, but no, way more exciting things,

Staying up all night is the best thing of all,
Then all the leaves and the children go wild,
When we get home sister Ella eats all her candy,
But I save the candy for my collection galore.

Shay Patel (9)
St Benedict's Junior School, London

I Am Me

I'm sporty, I'm funny, I'm mostly happy,
I'm friendly, I'm silly, I'm filled with curiosity,
I really love maths
But to me, humanity's a wrath.

I'm a super gigantic Potterhead
And one of my favourite colours is red.
I'm positive, I'm passionate, I'm creative and powerful,
I'm stressful, I'm depressed, I'm guilty and resentful.

Aiden Yihan Yuan (10)
St Benedict's Junior School, London

Rehmat Kaur

R ehmat, me... hello!
E xtremely awesome, that's me.
H ello again, if you come to me, all
M ake your house organised.
A world on its own! Oh! You don't know what I am talking about.
T alk to me!

K for kind Kaur!
A for awesome me!
U for umbrella, totally random!
R for Rehmat of course...

Rehmat Kaur Azad (8)
St Benedict's Junior School, London

This Is Me!

T his is excited, joyful me!
H alloween is my favourite time of the year because of the sweets.
I am so excited for our amazing school trip.
S ometimes I like to read.

I like when my dad picks me up.
S ometimes I like to lie down.

M y mum and me like to go to Ireland.
E veryone is so happy about the school trip.

Freya Kennedy-Alexander (8)
St Benedict's Junior School, London

This Is Me!

T his is a poem about the confident, busy me!
H ealthy I try to be when I am with my sister.
I t's time, for he says, "No!"
S andy beach and sand fort.

I s it time to have some fun with Owen?
S unny fun, but his mum is glum.

M atch Attax football cards he collects.
E lephant is my favourite animal.

Owen Byrne (7)
St Benedict's Junior School, London

This Is Me

My eyes are as brown as a tree,
I am happy as you can see.
I am fun and I am kind,
That's why I have a party in my mind.
I'm good at cricket,
And people always admit it.
I'm very cheeky,
That's why nobody can seek me.
I play the violin,
It fits perfectly under my chin.
I'm friendly, I'm brave,
Fish and chips I don't crave!

Vihaan Mathias (9)
St Benedict's Junior School, London

Sometimes

Sometimes I'm a dragon, valiant and strong
With shimmering scales, claws sharp and long.

Sometimes I'm a bug
Small and insignificant and weak.

Sometimes I'm a bird with sapphire and marigold wings
Swooping with a powerful flap.

Sometimes I'm a rose with scarlet petals
Until the spike of rejection burns them into flickering embers.

Reuben Adebutu (10)
St Benedict's Junior School, London

Oliver

T his is a poem about me!
H alloween is one of my favourite times of the year because I like ghosts,
I like playing chess every day,
S port is my favourite thing to do,

I really like cycling with my mum,
S ainsbury's is my second favourite shop,

M arch is my birthday,
E agles are my favourite animal.

Oliver Playle (7)
St Benedict's Junior School, London

Isobel

T his acrostic poem is about me.
H alloween is my favourite holiday, except for Christmas.
I sobel is my name.
S uperheroes are cool.

I 'm an exotic 7-year-old girl.
S ome people think I am funny.

M y favourite day is Friday because I get a treat dinner.
E ggs and sausages are my favourite breakfast.

Isobel Oldland (8)
St Benedict's Junior School, London

Yuika

T his is a poem about me!
H ena is my cousin's name.
I love people coming to my house for a play date.
S ometimes I like to go to the swimming pool.

I love all of my family members.
S ometimes I like to eat ice cream after swimming.

M aly is my older cousin's name.
E ishi is my smaller brother.

Yuika Naganuma (7)
St Benedict's Junior School, London

Jamie

J amie, like delicious, scrumptious jam on toast with butter.
A nd I have got the best, most kind, number one teacher in the world.
M y favourite, favourite thing to do is to play with my best friend, Leo.
I like to play with my Beyblade in my sick Battle Arena.
E nergetic and fast because I have a bit of sugar and I run a lot in the playground.

Jamie Marshall (7)
St Benedict's Junior School, London

This Is Me

T he people in my family are lovely to me,
H umanities is my favourite subject,
I love to play sports,
S ongs are my favourite.

I like instruments,
S nakes are my favourite animal because they are scary.

M y favourite thing is Beyblade,
E nergetic, confident and quick are words I will describe.

Leo Mehrabi (7)
St Benedict's Junior School, London

Gamer

I've been a gamer and I play tragic Minecraft.
I rock the wall with my edited Roblox ball.
I've raised up my budgie to talk like a man.
I write comic books within a second
And do dot-to-dot for hours.
If selfish gamers are going to hack me,
I'll have to get my revenge back on those proud people.
I am passionate about gaming and being a YouTuber.

John Khadouri (8)
St Benedict's Junior School, London

My Birthday

Today is the day!
And I'm so excited,
Everyone will shout *hooray!*
And we will sing together and play.
I will sing, shout and play about
Because it's my birthday today.
Everyone will eat together and we will
Sit together and when it's time I will
Say *goodbye.*
I will go home to celebrate
To finish off the day.

Luca Brathwaite (9)
St Benedict's Junior School, London

Aariyan

T his is a poem about me!
H i I am Aariyan and I am good at chess
I am good at art and like art too
S t Benedict's is my school

I like doing all types of art
S aturday is one of my favourite days of the week

M arch is when my brother's birthday is
E ggs are my favourite breakfast.

Aariyan Fofaria (7)
St Benedict's Junior School, London

Theo

T heo is my name
H ello fellow reader
I like Amazing Avengers
S words and Sandals is my favourite topic

I love reading interesting comic books
S uperThings are my favourite collectable figures

M y ancestors are famous Chinese Mauritian people
E xquisite sponge cake is super yummy.

Theo Joannou (7)
St Benedict's Junior School, London

I Am A...
A kennings poem

Tennis player
Basketball scorer
Football saver
Badminton smasher

Olive eater
Cookie muncher
Water chugger
Chocolate slasher

Snore monster
Teddy bear slayer
Master drooler
Pillow basher

Roblox player
Cliff dropper
Burger gobbler
Potato crusher
And finally...
A good friend.

Noah Khatibi (9)
St Benedict's Junior School, London

Archie

T his poem is an acrostic poem about me
H alloween is one of my favourite times of the year
I was born in 2016
S aturday is my favourite day

I love all of my family
S ausages and mash is one of my favourite meals

M y name is Archie
E ggs and bacon is one of my favourite foods.

Archie Hird (7)
St Benedict's Junior School, London

This Is Me

T his is the marvellous me.
H ealthy person I want to be.
I am from Iran, England and Ireland.
S ongs by Ed Sheeran I really love.

I love pizza and my favourite topping is margherita.
S ometimes, I am naughty.

M y headteacher is called Mr Simmons.
E nergetic boy, I really am.

Aiden Maugham (7)
St Benedict's Junior School, London

Mila

T his is an acrostic poem about me,
H andstands are my favourite thing to do,
I love painting too,
S ometimes I like playing football,

I ndigo is my favourite colour,
S and is my favourite thing to play with at the beach,

M ila is my name,
E agles are my favourite animals.

Mila Patel (7)
St Benedict's Junior School, London

Gaming

Gaming is really fun!
With games in which you make buns.
In Roblox, I'm Marshmallowmiao,
So come and find me now.
And don't be scared of hackers,
That report button is always there.
Minecraft is my number two,
And I have a house made of goo.
With only cubes which are very cool.

Do you like gaming?
I do!

Yunlie Li (8)
St Benedict's Junior School, London

Me And Papayas

Papayas are great things.
Me and papayas are great friends!
Papayas are great things, so I'm a papaya!
Because I'm a great thing!
We're all papayas!
Papayas are sweet, I'm sweet.
Papayas are cool like me, obviously.
What else?
Oh yeah, papayas have a name like me and...
They're just great, like me!

Olivia Oke (8)
St Benedict's Junior School, London

Magnificent Me!

I really like gymnastics,
When it comes to creativity, I'm very enthusiastic.
I have a little brother that's as jumpy as a kangaroo,
Maybe one day he will end up in a zoo.
Cake pops are a real treat,
They are so yummy to eat.
I really like dancing,
Maybe one day I'll learn to do prancing.

This is me!

Elysia Papathanasiou (9)
St Benedict's Junior School, London

Time

F intan is fun,
I s like a forgetful frog,
N ine next year,
T ime, why not nearer,
A nd I get ready,
N ight and day.

It is fun,
I don't know,
And they say,
Yes or no,
It will be like paradise,
With all the crowds,
I am so excited,
This is me!

Fintan Avella (8)
St Benedict's Junior School, London

Lydia

L ydia likes to have a bubbly, hot bath when it is cold
Y ou can find me at my house playing my new game
D o you like maths like me and are you quizzing?
I like drawing lots of great stuff that comes into my mind
A pples are my favourite fruit and carrots and cucumbers, I like them.

Lydia Johnson (7)
St Benedict's Junior School, London

Football

F ootball is the best
O wn goals are bad
O r you can score
T ackles can get you a yellow card
B ad tackles can get you a red card
A fter ninety minutes they look at the score
L ose or win, nobody knows
L eave the World Cup or win the Major Trophy.

Rufus Wilson (8)
St Benedict's Junior School, London

All About Me
A kennings poem

I am a...
Tennis player
Rugby watcher
A leaves supporter
Fishy swimmer

Fantastic learner
50 points earner
Bronze award taker
Best friend maker

WW2 explorer
Harry hater
Fighter watcher
Accurate bomber

And finally...
A natural encyclopedia.

Zak Vosser (9)
St Benedict's Junior School, London

Wolfie

T his is a poem about me!
H ello, I am Wolfie.
I like pizza.
S inging is my favourite thing to do.

I like to trick or treat.
S piders are my favourite insect.

M y birthday is on 25th June.
E ggs, I love, especially fried egg.

Wolfie Ashman (7)
St Benedict's Junior School, London

This Is Me
A kennings poem

I am a...

Chocolate eater
Cricket player
Deep sleeper
Strong gamer
Football watcher
Eco warrior
Outside survivor
Coke drinker
Sweet eater
Meme maker
Piano player
Problem solver
Fast swimmer
Happy winner
And finally
A maths completer.

Charlie Goodridge (10)
St Benedict's Junior School, London

This Is Me

I love the glowing sun
Because you can play all day and it's loads of fun
I like to run all day
It's joyful when you can play

I'm glamorous, confident and bright
And I can jump as high as a kite
I am also kind and caring
But I really don't like sharing!

Millie Scambler (10)
St Benedict's Junior School, London

Football

F riendly to my friends and family.
O rganised and helpful.
O ptimistic when playing football.
T errible at drawing.
B rilliant at football and sports.
A s fast as a cheetah.
L ove football and sports
L ike school and hobbies.

Afonso Gomes (8)
St Benedict's Junior School, London

I Love...

I love...
Bananas,
And watching Doctor Who,
It is so fun,
My favourite animal is a wolf,
They are so cute.

I love SpongeBob and Gary,
And I love football,
It is the best.

But I'm so scared of ghosts,
And very, very scared,
Of spiders!

Ashwin Shah (8)
St Benedict's Junior School, London

All About Me
A kennings poem

I am a...
Star Wars lover
Zelda gamer
TV watcher
Amazing reader

Burger eater
Food taster
Salad muncher
Apple cruncher

Fencing player
Football kicker
Basketball shooter
Rugby tackler

And finally...
A good learner!

Taran Khera (9)
St Benedict's Junior School, London

Who Am I?

Games player
Gaming god
Fencing player
Brick builder
Book reader
Electricity eater
School student
Bungee jumper
Fussy mother
Annoying sister
Lesson learner
Amazing abseiler
Cross-country runner
Meat muncher
Vegetation destroyer.

Raj Sidhu (10)
St Benedict's Junior School, London

I Am Me

A kennings poem

I am a...

Football player
Chocolate eater
Game winner
City hater
Money maker
Red lover
TikTok creator
Fast runner
Car lover
Fajita eater
Music listener
Potter hater
Hot dog craver

And finally a...
Superhero!

Jackson Harris (10)
St Benedict's Junior School, London

Actions
A kennings poem

Pet lover
Book reader
J2O guzzler
Climate saver
Hockey player
Dog owner
Eco warrior
Friendly neighbour
House leader
Active runner
Lasagne devourer
Horse rider
Powerful swimmer
People pleaser
And finally
Country traveller.

Alessia McQuillan Visintini (10)
St Benedict's Junior School, London

This Is Me

I am as happy as a kangaroo
I hope I am just like you.

I am a good goal-maker
But a horrible baker.

Some say I am like a bee
But I'm just me.

I have an annoying brother
But a kind mother.

Now this is me
Just let me be.

Rayan Serroukh (9)
St Benedict's Junior School, London

This Is Me
A kennings poem

English lover
Science studier
Relentless Robloxer
Marvellous Minecrafter
Speedy rock climber
Ferocious fencer
Enthusiastic about elephants
Lego master builder
Supreme Star Wars watcher
Great gamer
Silly swimmer
Cliff jumping lover.

Marcus Lee (10)
St Benedict's Junior School, London

This Is Me!
A kennings poem

Netballer
Staying-at-home-er

Dog lover
Party lover

Light sleeper
Sweet eater

Laughter
Giggler

Screener
Food eater

Homework hater
Hair straightener

Night awaker
Morning stretcher.

Carlotta Vannuccini (11)
St Benedict's Junior School, London

All About Me

In sport, I am the king
And football is my thing
I am a fierce rugby player
In taking a literal slayer

At piano, I am the best
I play all night and never take a rest

I'm friendly, I'm brave,
Fish and chips I don't crave.

Mark Pantea (10)
St Benedict's Junior School, London

This Is Me
A kennings poem

I am a...
TV lover
Loving sister
Light sleeper
Music admirer
Youtube watcher
Creative writer
Annoying little sister
Birthday lover
Family supporter
South Africa lover
Committed gamer
And finally a
Sports hater.

Letlotlo Wanjau (10)
St Benedict's Junior School, London

Me!
A kennings poem

I am a...
Deep reader
Powerful thinker
Good gamer
Movie watcher
Passionate rugby supporter
Positive eater
Bad sleeper
Creative drawer
Long talker
Country traveller
Chocolate scoffer
Because, after all, I am
Me!

Lucas Nossa (10)
St Benedict's Junior School, London

This Is Me!

Often time saver
Sometimes a money spender

Itself controller
Never a nice cleaner

A nice writer
Although not a nice reader

A fan of netball
But never a fan of hockey

A pencil snatcher
And a big yearner.

Lisa Stoilovska (10)
St Benedict's Junior School, London

This Is Me
A kennings poem

This is me
Sushi eater
Snow jumper
Monkey climber
Robbie Williams lover
Dance winner
Play thinker
Cat hugger
Beach swimmer
TV watcher
Holiday traveller
Sport ruler
Party bringer
London liver
Money earner.

Anastasia Norman (10)
St Benedict's Junior School, London

Who Am I?

Who am I?
A gaming god
A brick builder
A meat muncher
A Star Wars stormer
An amazing imaginative imagination
A kind, thoughtful person
A daydreamer
A dog wanter
A story seeker.

So, who am I?
I am *Zac!*

Zac Bernard (10)
St Benedict's Junior School, London

This Is Me!
A kennings poem

I am a...
Chocolate eater
Passionate rugby player
Fast swimmer
Early riser
Sporty competitor
Winter lover
Harlequins supporter
England rugby lover
Sushi scoffer
Powerful dreamer
And finally, I am a
Rugby lover.

George Knight (10)
St Benedict's Junior School, London

This Is Me
A kennings poem

I am a...
Flair-y footballer
Chocolate scoffer
Cake demolisher
Peace maker
Arsenal watcher
Dog lover
Kindness bringer
Friendship maker
Energetic musician
Passionate fencer
And finally...
An early riser!

Leandro Craigen (11)
St Benedict's Junior School, London

All About Me
A kennings poem

I am a...
Netball player
Hair braider
Cookie maker
Crisp eater
Book reader
Potter supporter
Story writer
Good diver
Perfect painter
Dedicated drawer
Clothes fashionista
And finally
A good helper.

Niamh Kelly (9)
St Benedict's Junior School, London

This Is Me
A kennings poem

I am a...
Cookie muncher,
Bread baker,
Food eater,
Pancake maker,

Hockey shooter,
Pen player,
Football kicker,
Netball bouncer,

Pretty painter,
Good drawer,
Party planner,
Fun sketcher.

Olivia Lucas-Garner (9)
St Benedict's Junior School, London

Birthday School!

I'm here, I'm there, I'm everywhere
I really care
My party is tomorrow
I'm turning 8 then 9
It is soon time
I'm in a new school
I'm really full of fuel
I'm so excited to
See you there!

Maryam Alnajjar (9)
St Benedict's Junior School, London

The Amazing Life Of Me
A kennings poem

Long runner,
Nature lover,
Eager reader,
Peace teacher,
Book reader,
Piano player,
Creative leader,
Mischief maker,
Rugby tackler,
Swim splasher,
Power climber,
Competitive bringer,
Who am I?

Aran Virdi (9)
St Benedict's Junior School, London

This Is Me

I like gymnastics and sport
It is the best
May is the month before my birthday

On Friday it is the best day
It is swimming day
Go and play today

Everybody likes break
Now it is time to say goodbye.

Imogen Tringali (7)
St Benedict's Junior School, London

This Is Me
A kennings poem

I am...
Easy waker
Sports player
Crazy goer
Tennis lover
Summer hater
Winter waiter
Nintendo player
Night stayer
Lazy worker
Joke teller
Piano player
And finally...
Movie watcher.

James Giles (10)
St Benedict's Junior School, London

I Am Me

A kennings poem

I am a...
Book reader
Skill keeper
Bed sleeper
Vehicle driver
Sport player
Food chomper
Late riser
Good diver
Car lover
Fencing fencer
Best gamer
And finally...
A good helper.

Nathaniel Hodge (9)
St Benedict's Junior School, London

This Is Me
A kennings poem

I am a...
Rugby hater
Football player
Mesmerising mathematician
Fantastic fencer
Rubik's cuber
June lover
Table tennis killer
Park lover
And last but not least
Liverpool lover.

Kayden Yip (10)
St Benedict's Junior School, London

All About Me

I like to be free
I like to be me
I'm very courageous
I'm also outrageous

I like to draw on boxes
I also like foxes
I like to be crazy
I'm also a bit lazy.

Maria Bizrah (8)
St Benedict's Junior School, London

I Wish...

That I could fly
And feed squirrels every day.

I am kind, lovely, and nice
But I am amazing as well.

I run quickly
And I am really excited for superb surprises.

Vivaan Agarwal (9)
St Benedict's Junior School, London

Who Am I

A kennings poem

I am a
Net smasher
Fast runner
Hard worker
Bar smasher
Back bender
Peace maker
Good seeker
Mischief maker
Early riser
And finally
Friend maker.

Frida Blanco (9)
St Benedict's Junior School, London

This Is Me
A kennings poem

I am a...
Lazy kid,
Early waker,
Tall guy,
Dog lover,
Crisp lover,
Fifa addict,
Football chugger,
Fanta lover,
Cereal killer.

Kenshiro Said (11)
St Benedict's Junior School, London

This Is Me
A kennings poem

I am a...

Confident swimmer
Creative drawer
Eager tennis player
Pasta eater
Inspired Olympic watcher
And finally a
Dog lover.

Freya Hughes (10)
St Benedict's Junior School, London

This Is Me
A kennings poem

Keyboard clicker
Mouse flicker
TV hogger
Sink clogger
Bedroom stayer
Video game player
Money keeper
Window peeper.

George Hacking (11)
St Benedict's Junior School, London

Me, Myself And I

I am kind, chatty and brave
I am ten, nearly eleven
And I really crave fun, enjoyment and the sun to come out
But when it comes, the clouds can't come about
My hair is as brown as an oak tree's bark
And I live quite close to the remarkable park
My eyes are like a bright blue flower
And my friends are as tall as the Eiffel Tower.

I am a
Party maker
Chocolate eater
Heavy sleeper
Good listener
Poem writer
Organiser
Fun inducer
And finally
An amazing learner.

This is me!

Annalise Sharpe (10)
Stanton Community Primary School, Stanton

The Story Of Me

I'm as fast as a bolting cheetah,
I'm as strong as a gorilla.
And if you come near me,
Then you'll be my roast dinner.

I eat a lot of herbs,
Although I'm more of a meat eater.
I play a game called Fifa,
I use mostly Mo Salah.

My favourite sport is football,
One of my four hobbies.
And when I grow up,
I might become a bobby.
But I think it is better to be,
My favourite hobby.

I'm a Brown, I'm young,
I'm still growing up.
And when I'm older,
I want to be a footballer.

I am Jesse Hendrix Brown
And this is me.

Jesse Brown (9)
Stanton Community Primary School, Stanton

Me

To create me, you will need:
600g happiness
A pinch of sadness
Two teaspoons of coolness
Four drops of friendliness
A clash of brightness
A slice of chicken pizza
And a sprinkle of me.

Now you need to:
Add the happiness and friendliness into a bowl with the coolness and stir together.
Next, add the pinch of sadness and the dash of brightness, and stir again.
Finally, add a slice of chicken pizza.
Cook until you see a smile, and add the sprinkle of me.
This is me!

Mia Preston (10)
Stanton Community Primary School, Stanton

My Favourite Animal
A riddle

Although it's an amphibian, it only lives in the sea,
It has pretty gills, and in Mexico it lives free,
When older, it eats dead rats, isn't that vile?
But at every age of its life, it can only smile,
In the wild, they're endangered, but as pets they're fine,
Their tales are so long that they look like a vine,
They are nearly blind,
But they are still kind,
What is it?

Answer: An axolotl.

Freddie Smith (11)
Stanton Community Primary School, Stanton

My Dog

He is a cute little Herbert, he is 100 miles an hour
He really has doggy superpowers.
He's brown, black and white
He does not put up a very good fight
But his cuddles were warm
After he was born.
He has brown eyes, he has warm fluffy ears
He makes everyone cry happy tears.
If you have seen a beagle, you know what I mean
This is my dog Herbert in a big lovely dream.

Joshua Smith Kerry (10)
Stanton Community Primary School, Stanton

This Is Me!

Tuesday in shorts and top,
I storm in the hall
Whilst catching the ball,
This is me!

Standing behind the wicket,
Gloved hand,
It's wicked.
This is me.

They made me captain,
Happy and proud.
I wowed the crowd.
This is me.

I'm at Lords,
In my dreams,
I'm in the England team.
This is me.

Albie Bryant-Howe (10)
Stanton Community Primary School, Stanton

Riddle

The animal is grey,
With rock-hard feet,
It can squash you,
It has a very, very long trunk,
With very small eyes,
It can run faster than you,
It can walk on all fours,
And eat you in *one* bite!
It can whack you with its trunk,
And it has very sharp teeth.
Did you guess what it is?

Answer: It's an elephant!

Dylan Policarpio (8)
Stanton Community Primary School, Stanton

What Am I? A Bird, A Fish, A Cat Or A Dog?

I am fast on four legs.
I can not lay eggs.
I can not fly fast and free.
I am nice to stroke and see.

People can ride me.
If I'm not wild and free.
A saddle and bridle sound okay.
Is that what I should say?

I can wear a shoe.
And a blanket too.
I can canter.
But I can't drink Fanta.
What am I?

Jessica Yeandle (10)
Stanton Community Primary School, Stanton

Climbing A Mountain As Me

I carve the path I walk on,
But I love the heat from the bath.
I work first, then I bathe all day long.
I can climb a mountain, sail across the sea,
But I love to see myself achieve my goal.
And at the top is the pot of gold that waits for me.
I am strong, I am brave, I am silly.
I can climb a mountain by myself,
I am unique!

Lilah Cross (9)
Stanton Community Primary School, Stanton

Me - The Rap

Funny, amazing
Love is what I'm craving.
I don't know what I'm saying
Lying on the grass, star gazing.

I can laugh, I can cry
I can always say goodbye.
I don't really know why
I can always wear my tie.

This is me
So you can see.
Always with my friends
The fun will never end.

Harry Cooper (10)
Stanton Community Primary School, Stanton

This Is Me

Add in:
Horse rider
Sprinkles
Happiness
Strength
Ice cream
Pizza
Challenges
Chocolate.

How to make me:
Add all the ingredients into a bowl.
Stir it all up and pour it into the tray.
Put it into the oven.
You have made me!

Darcey Marshall (8)
Stanton Community Primary School, Stanton

How To Create Me

What you will need:

10lbs of happiness
A pinch of angriness
10lbs of fun

How to make it:

Stir 10lbs of happiness
And add 10lbs of fun
And finally
Add in the pinch of angriness
And you're done!

This is me!

Layla Turner (9)
Stanton Community Primary School, Stanton

Memories

I love sharing memories,
I am a drama queen,
I love reading,
I have big, fierce dreams,
I am brave,
I am strong,
I am beautiful,
I am passionate,
I'm not frightened,
I am pleasant,
I am kind,
I am amazing,
This is me!

Ava-Leigh Russell Howllet (9)
Stanton Community Primary School, Stanton

This Is Me

I am strong
I am determined
When the sun comes out
I am always about
This is me
I am an early riser
A summer wisher
A chocolate eater
Waiting to disappear
My eyes are as blue as the sky
This is me.

Taylor Glass (10)
Stanton Community Primary School, Stanton

I Am Me
A kennings poem

I am an
Animal lover
Book reader
Wasp fleer
Football player
Bird watcher
Football watcher
Arsenal fan
Light sleeper
Swimmer
Prime drinker
Early riser
A funny person
Lovely person.

Reece Cannings (8)
Stanton Community Primary School, Stanton

This Is Me!

Chocolate is like a pool in my eyes,
I don't pay fines,
But I like cooking fries,
I love to buy,
But luckily, I am not a miner,
The thing that I dread,
Is getting out of bed.

Chelsea Dore (10)
Stanton Community Primary School, Stanton

This Is Me

I am...
Diving keeper
Friendly
Liker of Donnaruma
Unhelpful
Adorer of pizza
A lover of dirt tracks full of bikes
The chocolate slayer
The Prime lover
This is me.

Rex Cooper (10)
Stanton Community Primary School, Stanton

Me

A kennings poem

I am a
Chocolate eater
A good helper
Coleslaw eater
Late waker
Hard worker
Kind talker
Behaved
Friendly
Light sleeper
And finally
Passionate.

Caitlin Goodridge (9)
Stanton Community Primary School, Stanton

A Kennings Poem

A kennings poem

I am a...

Chocolate eater
Wasp avoider
Deep sleeper
Early riser
Smart boy
Strong boy
Funny joker
Crazy fun
And finally...
A good helper!

Finlay Ketcher (8)
Stanton Community Primary School, Stanton

This Is Me!

I'm cute
I'm big
I can't get under my bed
I'm a fast eater
I'm a light sleeper
I'm good at math
I have lots of energy!
This is me!

Freddie Olney (8)
Stanton Community Primary School, Stanton

My Favourite Animal

A creature of the mountains
As it is not nearly tame.
It has fur,
But it has no feathers.
It can run,
But cannot be fun.

Answer: Mountain goat.

Bailey Daniel Thomas Hazelton (10)
Stanton Community Primary School, Stanton

Me

A kennings poem

I am an ice cream eater
Sport player
Dancer
Animal lover
Mess maker
Joke cracker
Bold and brave
Energetic and happy
I am unique!
I am me!

Isabelle Steed (9)
Stanton Community Primary School, Stanton

This Is Me!
A kennings poem

I am a
Sports player
Football player
Food eater
Good helper
Kind person
Early riser
Football superstar
Great sleeper
This is me!

James Hope (10)
Stanton Community Primary School, Stanton

I Am A...
A kennings poem

I am a...
Swifty
Risky
Summer wisher
Biscuit eater
Deep sleeper
Good friend
And finally...
Me!

Esmie O'Reilly (11)
Stanton Community Primary School, Stanton

My Inspiration

They ride so long.
They're truly the world.
She works so hard
To achieve her goal.

I love her so much,
She is so good at what she does.
She inspires me so much
When we ride so long.

When she falls, she gets back on.
She doesn't give up
Unless she is broken.
She is the best in the world.

She lost one another.
She loves Lola in the world.
She loves me so much.
She would die for me.

She is the best in the world.
I would not trade her.
She helps one another
By helping me ride.

Bonnie Jo Randall Jackson (10)
Stapleford Abbotts Primary School, Stapleford Abbotts

I Like Nuggets

I like chicken nuggets
I think it truly describes me
Crispy and tender and juicy as well
Whenever I eat one, I'm filled with glee.

Dip it in sauce, ketchup is best
But others are yummy and tasty
Like barbecue, curry sauce and others too
Nuggets are grat, don't put them to waste

McDonald's and Popeye's and KFC too
Burger King and Wendy's are fine
All of these nuggets are very good
When I take a bite I'm on cloud 9.

Lucas Pitcher (9)
Stapleford Abbotts Primary School, Stapleford Abbotts

What I Am

A mazing
V ery good at dancing
A wesome.

Chocolate, I love chocolate, it is my second favourite dessert
My favourite is a brownie
Watching Moriah Elizabeth, she is so good at arts and crafts.

F is for fantastic
A is for amazing
M is for mastermind
I is for intelligent
L is for love
Y is for you are amazing.

Ava-Lea Brimacombe (9)
Stapleford Abbotts Primary School, Stapleford Abbotts

This Is Me

I am small,
I am not tall.
I have hazel eyes,
I never tell lies.
I am very kind,
I answer all my questions with my mind.
I am very cool,
But some people want to rule.
I am me,
I always will be.
Sometimes, I am feeling as cold as ice,
But overall, I am very nice.
The clouds are above,
I am full of love.
My nickname is Si-Si,
And this is me!

Sienna Ippoliti (8)
Stapleford Abbotts Primary School, Stapleford Abbotts

All About Talulah-Rose

T o do as a hobby is gymnastics
A rt is relaxing and I love it
L ove ice cream
U nbelievable friend
L ove cake
A rt is hard
H ow do I hang upside down with no hands?

R uby is my best friend in the world
O ctopus is slimy
S ometimes I like school
E lephants are my favourite animal.

Talulah-Rose Adams-Smith (8)
Stapleford Abbotts Primary School, Stapleford Abbotts

Story Of Dervis

D odgeball is my favourite.
E veryone calls me cute because I have freckles
R eading is the best.
V R is the future.
I love helping my teachers.
S uperhero is what I will become.

R oni is my name.
O n my way to the future.
N o one can stop me.
I will embroider my name to this world.

Dervis Maraslioglu (7)
Stapleford Abbotts Primary School, Stapleford Abbotts

All About Me!

W onderful Winnie
I ndependent with my work
N ice to all of my friends
N ever giving up
I 'm not like other girls, I love football
E legant in dancing

D ogs are my favourite animal
U nbelievable
F unny joke teller
F abulous
Y ou are awesome no matter what.

Winnie Duffy (10)
Stapleford Abbotts Primary School, Stapleford Abbotts

Be You

Hello, my name is Teddy,
I am kind and sweet
I have got lots of friends called
Denny, Riley, Jude.

I have the best school
It is called
Stapleford Abbots
Primary School Academy.

This is what my name represents:

- **T** rue friend
- **E** asy going
- **D** elicate
- **D** ecent
- **Y** ours.

Teddy McAniskey (10)
Stapleford Abbotts Primary School, Stapleford Abbotts

Kindness

Kindness is key,
Kindness is smiles,
Kindness you can't see,
Kindness can go miles,

Kindness is togetherness,
Kindness is all we want,
Kindness can be a mess,
Kindness sometimes can't,

Kindness you will see,
Kindness is always key,
Kindness will always be,
Kindness is me.

Olivia Pitcher (11)
Stapleford Abbotts Primary School, Stapleford Abbotts

The

I love to be kind and helpful
S ometimes, I love school
L ike to help
A ll day, I love to be kind

W hen people come round, they play with my pets
E lephants are my favourite animal
S iener is my best friend
T alulah is my friend.

Isla West (8)
Stapleford Abbotts Primary School, Stapleford Abbotts

I Am...

I am kind,
I will achieve my goal and find,
I am ginger,
I'm sneaky like a ninja,
I'm very amusing,
I'm not worth accusing,
I can be as quiet as a mouse,
Or like a monkey in a house,
I'm good at video games,
But I also play football as it's not as lame.

Oliver Dockerill (9)
Stapleford Abbotts Primary School, Stapleford Abbotts

Cauã's Recipe

Cauã is here it's time to teach his recipe
His recipe is as fun as toys
Now it is time to cook
First to add is kindness
And then there is love
And well don't forget family is important
After here comes fastness
But don't forget my favourite thing is maths!

Cauã Santos (8)
Stapleford Abbotts Primary School, Stapleford Abbotts

This Is Me

I 'm independent
S trong and sometimes sad
L aughter inside of me
A nd happiness inside of me

R hythm inside of me
A lso I'm intelligent
Y ou, me and my friends are besties, my best friend is Kyla, she came to my birthday.

Isla Ray Hartley (7)
Stapleford Abbotts Primary School, Stapleford Abbotts

All About Freddie!

F avourite animal is a giraffe...
R eally loves his family...
E xcited to visit London at Christmas...
D oing art makes me happy...
D ogs make me feel calm...
I ncredible at maths...
E xcellent at swimming...

Freddie Jake Goddard (10)
Stapleford Abbotts Primary School, Stapleford Abbotts

Myself

O n task and focused.
L earning and enthusiastic.
I n maths, I'm really interested.
V ipers I love because it's about things.
I 'm independent in reading.
A lways happy and overjoyful.

Olivia Carle (7)
Stapleford Abbotts Primary School, Stapleford Abbotts

All About Me, Ellie

- **E** xcited to watch Lilo and Stitch movie.
- **L** ikely to have Stitch teddies.
- **L** ove Stitch and friend and family
- **I** 'm likely to have a friend.
- **E** xcited to go back to school and have new friends.

Ellie Eastwell (8)
Stapleford Abbotts Primary School, Stapleford Abbotts

Elsie-May

E legant Elsie
L ovely and kind
S uper smart
I love animals
E xcellent and helpful

M arvellous me
A lways amazing
Y ou matter!

Elsie-May Mesher (9)
Stapleford Abbotts Primary School, Stapleford Abbotts

This Is Me

R eally love tigers.
O h, I really love pizza.
S ometimes, I like to go to the park.
I love my cousin Isabella.
E verything is the best, every food is really yummy.

Rosie Violet Rawson (8)
Stapleford Abbotts Primary School, Stapleford Abbotts

This Is Me

J oyful and full of energy
O nly plays football
N ice and helpful
N ot allowed to kick a football in my house
Y oung and always kind.

Jonny Ansett (7)
Stapleford Abbotts Primary School, Stapleford Abbotts

This Is Me

J oyful smiles
E specially smart
N ever late
S uper significant
O fficially fast
N otoriously observant

Jenson Man (9)
Stapleford Abbotts Primary School, Stapleford Abbotts

This Is Me

R esilient and special.
I ndependent and smart.
L ucky and nice.
E asy going.
Y oung but kind.

Riley Van Haaren (10)
Stapleford Abbotts Primary School, Stapleford Abbotts

This Is Me

O wen loves football
W hen I play it makes my day
E very day I like to play
N o bullies get in my way.

Owen (8)
Stapleford Abbotts Primary School, Stapleford Abbotts

This Is Me

M indful and careful, loving.
I ndependent in English and all sorts of writing subjects.
A rtful and creative.

Mia (8)
Stapleford Abbotts Primary School, Stapleford Abbotts

Ayla

A mazing me
Y ellow is my favourite colour
L ovely me
A ctive and fun.

Ayla Sonmez (9)
Stapleford Abbotts Primary School, Stapleford Abbotts

Friendship

I am kind to those who need some kindness
Friendship is the word.
In case you have not heard.
I am the top friend in all the class.
Friendship will make the school a better place.
No one should have best friends
It will make others feel upset
Instead, we should all connect as a school.

Beatrix Johnson (7)
The Coppice Primary School, Hollywood

YOUNG WRITERS INFORMATION

We hope you have enjoyed reading this book – and that you will continue to in the coming years.

If you're the parent or family member of an enthusiastic poet or story writer, do visit our website www.youngwriters.co.uk/subscribe and sign up to receive news, competitions, writing challenges and tips, activities and much, much more! There's lots to keep budding writers motivated!

If you would like to order further copies of this book, or any of our other titles, then please give us a call or order via your online account.

Young Writers
Remus House
Coltsfoot Drive
Peterborough
PE2 9BF
(01733) 890066
info@youngwriters.co.uk

Join in the conversation!
Tips, news, giveaways and much more!

 YoungWritersUK    YoungWritersCW    youngwriterscw

 Scan me to watch the This Is Me video!